T0375932

Native Americans

The Pueblo

Barbara A. Gray-Kanatiiosh

ABDO Publishing Company

visit us at
www.abdopub.com

Published by ABDO Publishing Company, 4940 Viking Drive, Suite 622, Edina, Minnesota 55435. Copyright © 2002 by Abdo Consulting Group, Inc. International copyrights reserved in all countries. No part of this book may be reproduced in any form without written permission from the publisher.

Printed in the United States.

Illustrations: David Kanietakeron Fadden
Interior Photos: Corbis
Editors: Bob Italia, Tamara L. Britton, Kate A. Conley, Kristin Van Cleaf
Art Direction & Maps: Neil Klinepier

Library of Congress Cataloging-in-Publication Data

Gray-Kanatiiosh, Barbara A., 1963-
    The Pueblo / Barbara A. Gray-Kanatiiosh.
      p. cm. -- (Native Americans)
    Includes index.
    Summary: An introduction to the food, homes, clothing, crafts, and social life and customs of the Pueblo Indians, a tribe of the southwestern United States.
    ISBN 1-57765-606-7
    1. Pueblo Indians--Juvenile literature. [1. Pueblo Indians. 2. Indians of North America--Southwest, New.] I. Title.
II. Native Americans (Edina, Minn.)

E99.P9 G665 2002
978. 9'004974--dc21

2001058983

About the Author: Barbara A. Gray-Kanatiiosh, JD

Barbara Gray-Kanatiiosh, JD, is an Akwesasne Mohawk. She has a Juris Doctorate from Arizona State University, where she was one of the first recipients of ASU's special certificate in Indian Law. She is currently pursuing a Ph.D. in Justice Studies at ASU and is focusing on Native American issues. Barbara works hard to educate children about Native Americans through her writing and Web site where children may ask questions and receive a written response about the Haudenosaunee culture. The Web site is: www.peace4turtleisland.org

Illustrator: David Kanietakeron Fadden

David Kanietakeron Fadden is a member of the Akwesasne Mohawk Wolf Clan. His work has appeared in publications such as *Akwesasne Notes, Indian Time*, and the *Northeast Indian Quarterly*. Examples of his work have also appeared in various publications of the Six Nations Indian Museum in Onchiota, NY. His work has also appeared in "How The West Was Lost: Always The Enemy," produced by Gannett Production which appeared on the Discovery Channel. David's work has been exhibited in Albany, NY; the Lake Placid Center for the Arts; Centre Strathearn in Montreal, Quebec; North Country Community College in Saranac Lake, NY; Paul Smith's College in Paul Smiths, NY; and at the Unison Arts & Learning Center in New Paltz, NY.

Contents

Where They Lived

The Pueblo Native Americans live in the same homelands they lived in for a thousand years. The Pueblo are made up of 21 tribes. These tribes include the Zuni of western New Mexico and the Hopi of northeastern Arizona. They share similar ways of life, ceremonial beliefs, and geographic regions.

The name *Pueblo* comes from the Spanish word for town. The Pueblo's ancestors are the **Anasazi**. They lived in the same region more than a thousand years ago.

The many Pueblo tribes do not speak the same language. There are three Pueblo dialects: Tiwa, Tewa, and Towa. These dialects belong to the Tanoan, Keresean, and Zunian language families.

The Pueblo live in permanent village communities in the southwestern United States. These communities are built atop **mesas** near rivers.

Most Pueblo village communities are located in the Rio Grande valley, in present-day New Mexico. The Pueblo homelands have canyons, deserts, mountain ranges, high mountain peaks, and mesas.

The Rio Grande valley in New Mexico

The Pueblo Homelands

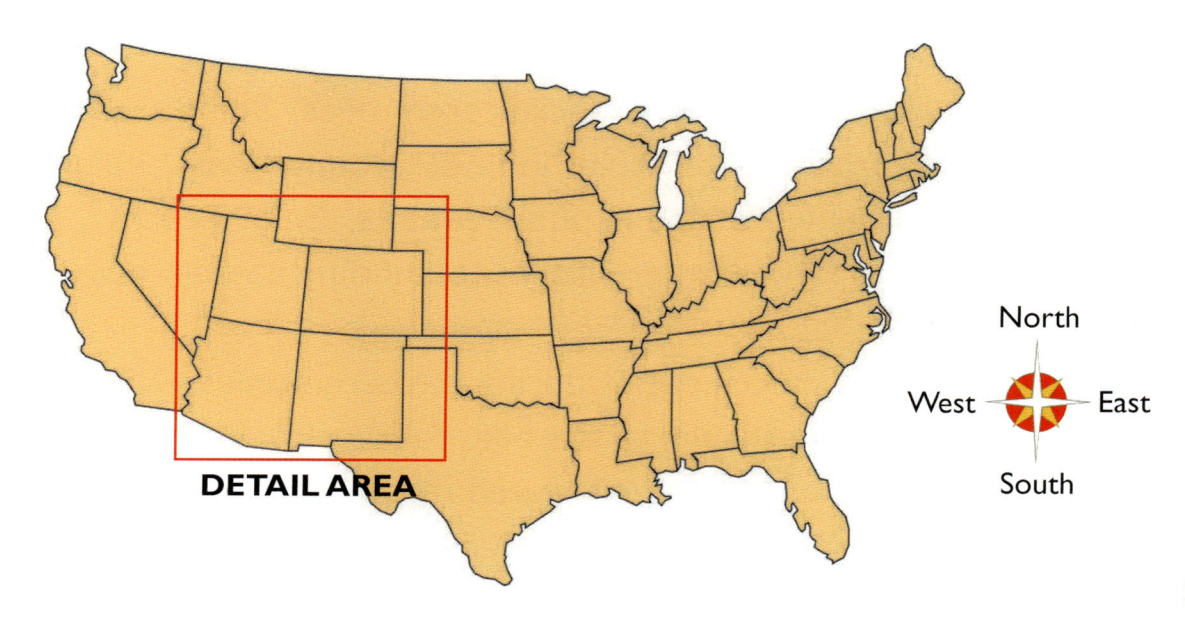

DETAIL AREA

North

West — East

South

Society

Pueblo society was held together by kinship ties called **clans**. Some Pueblo tribes had more than 20 clans. Pueblo clans had strong spiritual beliefs. They believed their duty was to care for their environment.

Each Pueblo village had both political and spiritual leaders. There were chiefs, assistant chiefs, and law enforcers. The villages also had priests and medicine people who conducted ceremonies and healed people.

Pueblo villages often held special ceremonies. Some sacred societies held private ceremonies in underground **kivas**. Many other ceremonies were held in public **plazas**. Before each ceremony, criers ran to other villages to announce when it would take place.

Each clan had special duties during the ceremonies. At these times, the clans gave thanks to the Natural World. The Pueblo believed ceremonies of thanks showed respect and maintained the world's balance.

A Pueblo village

Food

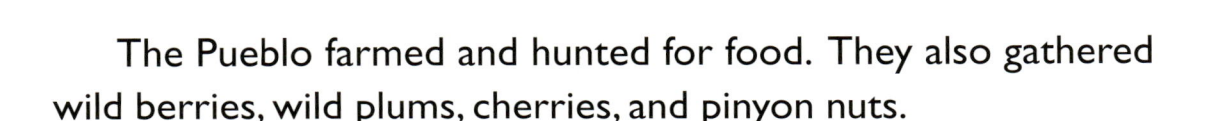

The Pueblo farmed and hunted for food. They also gathered wild berries, wild plums, cherries, and pinyon nuts.

Because water was scarce, the Pueblo practiced **dry farming**. They often planted crops in **washes** that filled with water from snowmelt and summer rains. The Pueblo also watered their fields with river and spring water.

Most of a village's food supply came from its corn fields. The Pueblo used digging sticks to plant corn. First, they pushed the stick about 12 inches (31 cm) into the ground. Then Pueblo farmers placed several corn seeds in each hole. The deep holes made sure the new plants' roots would be close to underground water.

The Pueblo also grew beans, squash, and melons. Later, Europeans introduced new foods to the Pueblo. Then they grew peaches, apricots, and grapes, too. As the crops grew, Pueblo farmers tended to the gardens using long-handled hoes with animal-bone blades.

Pueblo hunters also supplied the villages with food. They hunted for large game such as deer, bighorn sheep, pronghorn, and bison with bows and arrows. They hunted smaller game such as rabbits, squirrels, wild turkeys, quail, ducks, and doves with handwoven **snares**. Eventually, the Pueblo raised their own sheep and cattle.

1. A Pueblo man uses a digging stick. 2. A digging stick with a foot rest. 3. A hoe made from an animal's shoulder blade.

Homes

Pueblo women built their families' houses. Walls were made of stone and sandstone set in **adobe** mortar and covered with a thick layer of mud and clay. The roofs and floors were made of log beams covered with brush, grass, and a thick layer of clay. The thick walls and roof kept the houses cool in the summer and warm in the winter.

Inside each house, a long bench stretched along one wall. Another wall had three stone boxes. Each box contained a grindstone called a *metate* (muh-TAH-tay). The women knelt at the boxes and ground corn on the *metates* for hours each day.

Pueblo homes were built close together and on top of each other like apartment buildings. The Pueblo lived in the top story, and used the bottom story for storage. Wooden ladders were used to move from story to story. Each house connected to an outdoor **plaza** and the **kiva**. Women from nearby homes shared beehive-shaped ovens to bake breads.

Pueblo homes

Clothing

The Pueblo wore both deerskin and cloth clothing. The men wove cloth from cotton fibers and colored it with plant and **mineral** dye.

Women and girls often wore rectangular dresses. Each dress was made from one long strip of cloth. The cloth wrapped around the body and over the right shoulder. The left shoulder was left uncovered. A **sash** tied around the waist held the dress in place.

Men and boys wore woven shirts, **kilts** or **breechcloths**, and **buckskin** leggings. Men also wrapped sashes around their waists. Sometimes men wore a sash across their chest that also tied at the waist.

Women wore moccasins with deerskin ankle wraps. They often rubbed the moccasins with white clay, which made them glisten. Men wore brown, ankle-high moccasins with light-colored soles. Pueblo moccasin soles came up all around the moccasin, like the sole on a rubber boot. The Pueblo also wore sandals woven from yucca plant leaves.

In the winter, the Pueblo wore rabbit fur moccasins. They also wrapped woven blankets and fur robes around their shoulders to keep warm.

The Pueblo decorated their clothing with colors and symbols that represented nature and their **culture**. And they wore jewelry made from shells and turquoise.

Men wore their hair long, with short bangs. They often tied their long hair into a folded bun. Women wore their hair long. Unmarried women often wore their hair in a butterfly style. To make this style, they wrapped their hair around wooden forms.

A Pueblo family in traditional dress

13

Crafts

The Pueblo were skilled pottery makers. The Pueblo used pottery for storing food, holding water, and cooking.

To make a pot, the potters gathered the clay found under large slabs of rock on the **mesas**. They then strengthened the clay with a mix of stones and ground up pieces of old pots.

The potters rolled the clay into long, snakelike coils. Then they wound the coils in circles on top of each other until the pot was the desired size and shape. The potters used a flat stone or piece of gourd to blend together the coils until the pot had a smooth finish.

The Pueblo left the smooth pots in the sun to dry. Then they polished the dried pots with a stone. The Pueblo painted designs on the pots with brushes made from thin pieces of yucca stalks. They made paints from ground stones. After painting the pots, the potters **fired** them in a sandpit to make the pots stronger.

A Pueblo pottery maker

Family

Family was very important to the Pueblo. A Pueblo family consisted of the entire **clan**. Pueblo clans were matrilinear. This means that children belonged to their mother's clan. And a clan's women owned its gardens, homes, and possessions.

Because clan members were related, the Pueblo were not allowed to marry someone in their own clan. When a Pueblo couple decided to marry, the groom and his male relatives wove white wedding clothes for the bride. The bride and her female relatives ground corn for the wedding feast.

On their wedding day, the bride and groom took a pinch of corn meal. They walked to the east end of the **mesa**. Together they breathed in the corn meal and tossed it up to meet the rising sun. They prayed together and returned to the village a married couple. Then the couple moved into the bride's home.

Men hunted, made tools from bone and stone, and prepared the fields for planting. Women prepared the seeds for planting. They tended the children and prepared the meals. They also made pottery and baskets.

A Pueblo girl brings a boy some piki bread. If he shares it with his males relatives, it means the boy accepts the girl's marriage proposal.

Children

Pueblo parents carried their babies on **cradleboards**. Sometimes the baby's relatives tied the cradleboard to the ceiling with yucca ropes. While the women did their chores, the babies could swing. Babies stayed on their cradleboards until they were about a year old, and began learning to walk.

Children learned the Pueblo way of life from their **clan**. They learned about **kachinas** and the ceremonial dances and songs. They also learned how to make pottery and carve kachinas.

Children learned to offer a prayer to the rising sun at dawn. For this prayer, the boys and girls left corn pollen or meal outside their doors. The corn and prayer gave thanks for the new day.

Girls worked with their female relatives. They learned to grind corn, make corn mush and bread, and care for the children. Girls sometimes made and played with toy **adobe** homes, clay dolls, and small cradleboards. They also played with kachina dolls. The dolls taught the girls about the many different kachinas.

Boys worked with their male relatives. They went to the fields and learned to plant crops with digging sticks. They learned where to plant the fields so that the rain would water the corn. Boys also learned how to make bows and arrows. And they learned how to make and mend tools.

Pueblo children played running games that kept their bodies healthy. They also played darts. They made the darts from dried corncobs. Each cob had a sharp stick in one end and hawk feathers in the other end. The children threw the darts at a ring-shaped target.

A Pueblo mother and daughter pick berries.

Myths

The Pueblo emergence story tells how humans came to this world. The story teaches that humans have the duty to take care of the environment.

A long time ago, Dawa and Spider Woman created humans. They gave the humans instructions on how to pray and take care of the land. In return, humans would have enough resources to eat, clothe themselves, and be happy.

As time went on, the humans forgot to pray and care for the land. As punishment, the First World was destroyed. Humans were then given a second chance. The humans again forgot their original instructions, and the Second World was destroyed. The humans were given another chance and lived in the Third World. But again the humans forgot to live as they had been taught.

Dawa told the men to go down into the **kivas** and pray for a new place to live. As they prayed, different animals visited them. These animals later became the Pueblo **clans**. Soon the men saw an opening above them, but could not reach it. A reed was planted. The huge reed grew tall enough to reach the opening.

The Pueblo climbed up the reed and entered into the Fourth World. The *sipapu*, the opening, is said to be located in the Grand Canyon, in Arizona. The Pueblo traveled from the *sipapu* in many directions before settling where they live today.

The Pueblo enter the Fourth World.

War

The Pueblo were peaceful people. Their spiritual beliefs taught them to live in peace with other people and the environment. When the Pueblo did go to war, it was usually to defend themselves. Before going to war, Pueblo men sometimes painted their bodies. To protect themselves, they carried shields made from bison **hide**.

Tribes such as the Apache and Navajo raided the Pueblo villages. These tribes stole corn and captured women and children. They sold the captive women and children as slaves.

To defend themselves against these raids, the Pueblo used clubs, stone knives, and bows and arrows. They defended themselves with the wooden war clubs and stone knives when fighting in close contact. They used the bows and arrows when they were fighting from a distance. Some Pueblo warriors may have dipped their arrowheads in rattlesnake **venom**. The venom made the arrows more deadly.

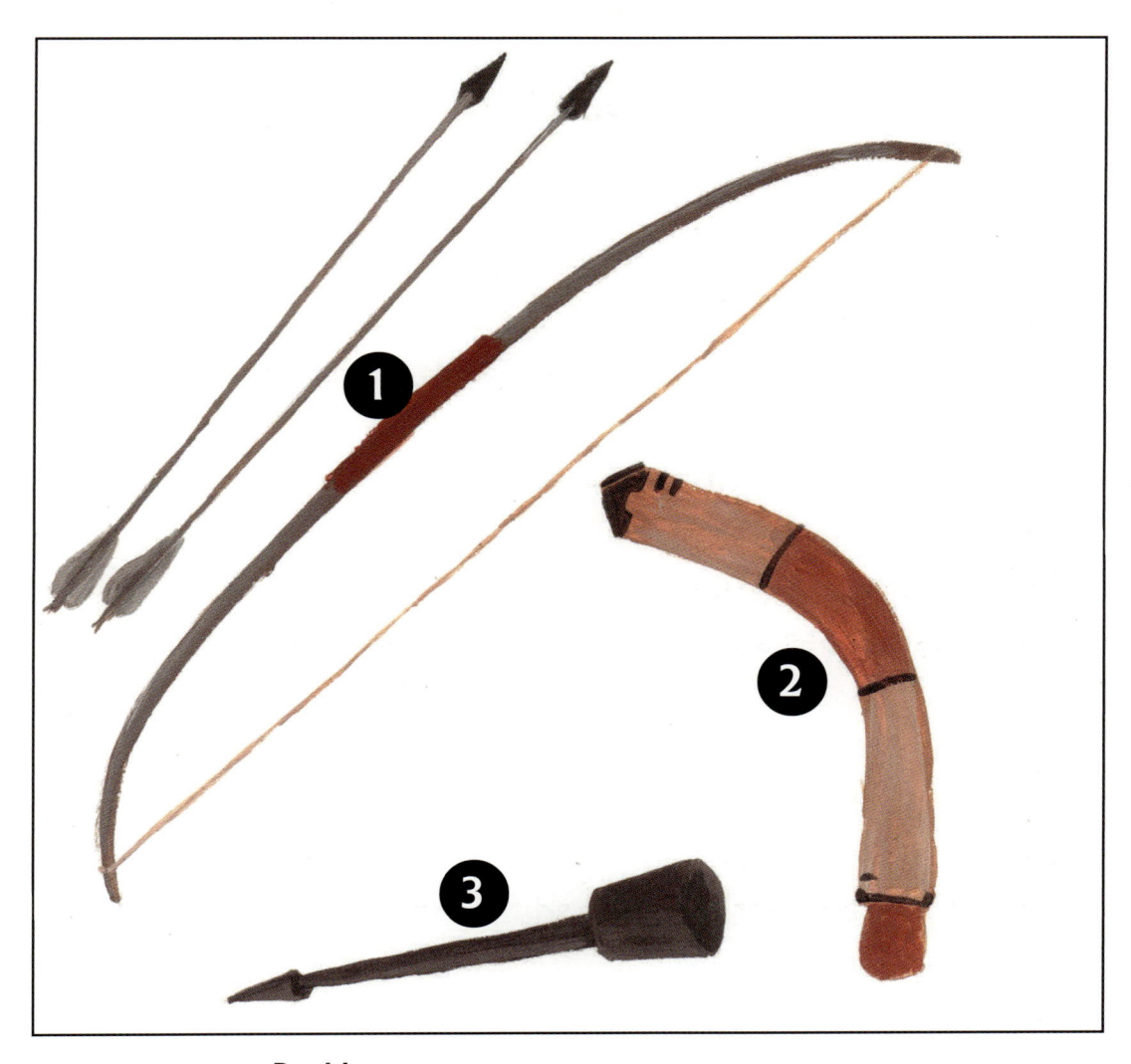

Pueblo weapons:
1. Bow and arrows 2. War club 3. Stone knife

Contact with Europeans

In 1539, Friar Marcos de Niza ventured into Zuni Lands. He saw the Zuni villages from a distance. He thought the villages were the legendary Seven Cities of Cibola, which many Spaniards believed were made of gold.

In 1540, Francisco Vásquez de Coronado came to the southwest looking for the Seven Cities of Cibola. But when Coronado came to the Pueblo villages, he saw there was no gold.

In 1598, San Juan Oñate and other Spaniards came to the Pueblo lands. His goal was to build **missions** and convert the Pueblo to Christianity. The Spaniards outlawed the Pueblo ceremonial practices and dances. This threatened the Pueblo's **culture**.

In 1680, the Pueblo revolted against the Spaniards. Many Pueblo villages attacked the Spanish in the revolt. The Pueblo were successful, and the Spaniards fled. But they returned later, in 1692.

A Pueblo man approaches a Spanish mission.

In 1848, Mexico and the United States signed the Treaty of Guadalupe Hidalgo. The treaty made the Pueblo homelands property of the U.S. government.

Popé

Popé (poh-PAY) was born in about 1630. He was a San Juan Pueblo religious and political leader. His real name was Popyn, which means Ripe Squash in the Tewa language. Today, he is known as Popé, or El Popé, because that is how the Spaniards recorded his name.

In his tribe, Popé was an assistant to the war captain. He helped with ceremonial dances and village socials. Later, he was made a war captain. This title was an honor with much responsibility.

In the late 1500s, the Spanish invaded Pueblo lands. During Popé's lifetime, the Spaniards made the Pueblo work as slaves. They made the Pueblo give up their own beliefs and convert to Christianity.

The Spaniards made laws to prevent the Pueblo from performing their traditional dances and ceremonies. They arrested, whipped, or even killed the Pueblo for practicing their beliefs.

Popé was one of those punished. He knew action was needed to protect his people and their **culture**. So Popé sent runners to all the Pueblo villages. The runners brought a message that there would soon be a massive revolt against the Spaniards.

The runners left a deerskin tied with knots at each village. Each knot represented the number of days to the start of the revolt. On August 10, 1680, many Pueblo villages united against the Spaniards in the Pueblo Revolt. They succeeded in driving the Spanish from Pueblo lands.

Popé died in 1688. He was a brave man who fought for his people and culture.

Popé

 The Pueblo Today

From the 1920s to today, land claims and water rights have been important issues for the Pueblo people. The Pueblo have fought hard for the return of lands that were illegally taken from them.

In the 1930s, the United States passed the Indian Reorganization Act (IRA). The IRA replaced the Pueblo's traditional form of government with governments that had **constitutions**.

In 1970, President Richard Nixon returned a piece of land to the Pueblo. This land included Blue Lake. Blue Lake is sacred to the Taos Pueblo. The U.S. government had taken the land that contained Blue Lake in 1906, as part of Carson National Forest. The Taos had fought for almost 70 years for the return of the sacred lake.

Today, the Pueblo are working to protect their environment, language, and **culture**. Tourism has become an important part of the Pueblo's **economy**. Tourists come to buy Pueblo crafts such

Individual houses nestle together to form Taos Pueblo, which has been inhabited for nearly 700 years.

as pottery, jewelry, and paintings. One of today's most famous Pueblo potters is Maria Martinez. She invented a style of pottery called black-on-black ware.

Today, there are Pueblo in many fields of work. Pueblo are doctors, lawyers, and artists. Many serve in the armed forces. Some served as **code talkers** during World War II. Two famous Pueblo writers are Leslie Marmon Silko and Dr. Alfonso Ortiz. Silko is a Laguna Pueblo. Ortiz is San Juan Pueblo and an **anthropologist**. Robert Mirabal is a Taos Pueblo musician, songwriter, and entertainer.

Glossary

adobe - a brick or building material of sun-dried earth and straw.

Anasazi - prehistoric Native Americans who lived in the southwestern United States, especially in what is now the Four Corners area, where Colorado, Utah, New Mexico, and Arizona meet.

anthropologist - a person who studies the origin, nature, and destiny of human beings.

breechcloth - a piece of hide or cloth, usually worn by men, that was wrapped between the legs and tied with a belt around the waist.

buckskin - a soft leather made of the skin of a buck.

clan - a group of families in a community that has a common ancestor.

code talkers - small groups of Native Americans who served in the United States armed forces in World War I (1914-1918) and World War II (1939-1945). Code talkers developed and used codes in Native American languages to send secret messages.

constitution - the laws that govern a country.

cradleboard - a flat board used to hold a baby. It could be carried on the mother's back or hung from a tree so that the baby could see what was going on.

culture - the customs, arts, and tools of a nation or people at a certain time.

dry farming - farming on nonirrigated land by planting drought-resistant crops and turning under soil wet with dew or rain.

economy - the way a colony, city, state, or nation uses its money, goods, and natural resources.

fire - to treat pottery with heat to make it stronger.

hide - an animal skin that is often thick and heavy.

kachina - an ancestral spirit of the Hopi and other Pueblo Native Americans.

kilt - a knee-length garment worn by men.

kiva - a ceremonial structure that is usually round and partly underground.

mesa - a flat-topped hill or mountain with steep sides.

mineral - an element, such as gold or silver, that is obtained by digging in the earth.

mission - a center or headquarters for religious work.

plaza - a public square in a city or town.

sash - a band worn about the waist or over one shoulder.

snare - a trap often consisting of a noose for catching birds or mammals.

venom - a poison produced by some animals and insects, usually introduced into a victim by a bite or sting.

wash - the bed of a stream that is usually dry, but that runs with water after a rain.

Web Sites

The Pueblo of Santa Ana
http://www.santaana.org/

The All Indian Pueblo Council
http://www.aipcinc.com/

These sites are subject to change. Go to your favorite search engine and type in Pueblo for more sites.

Index